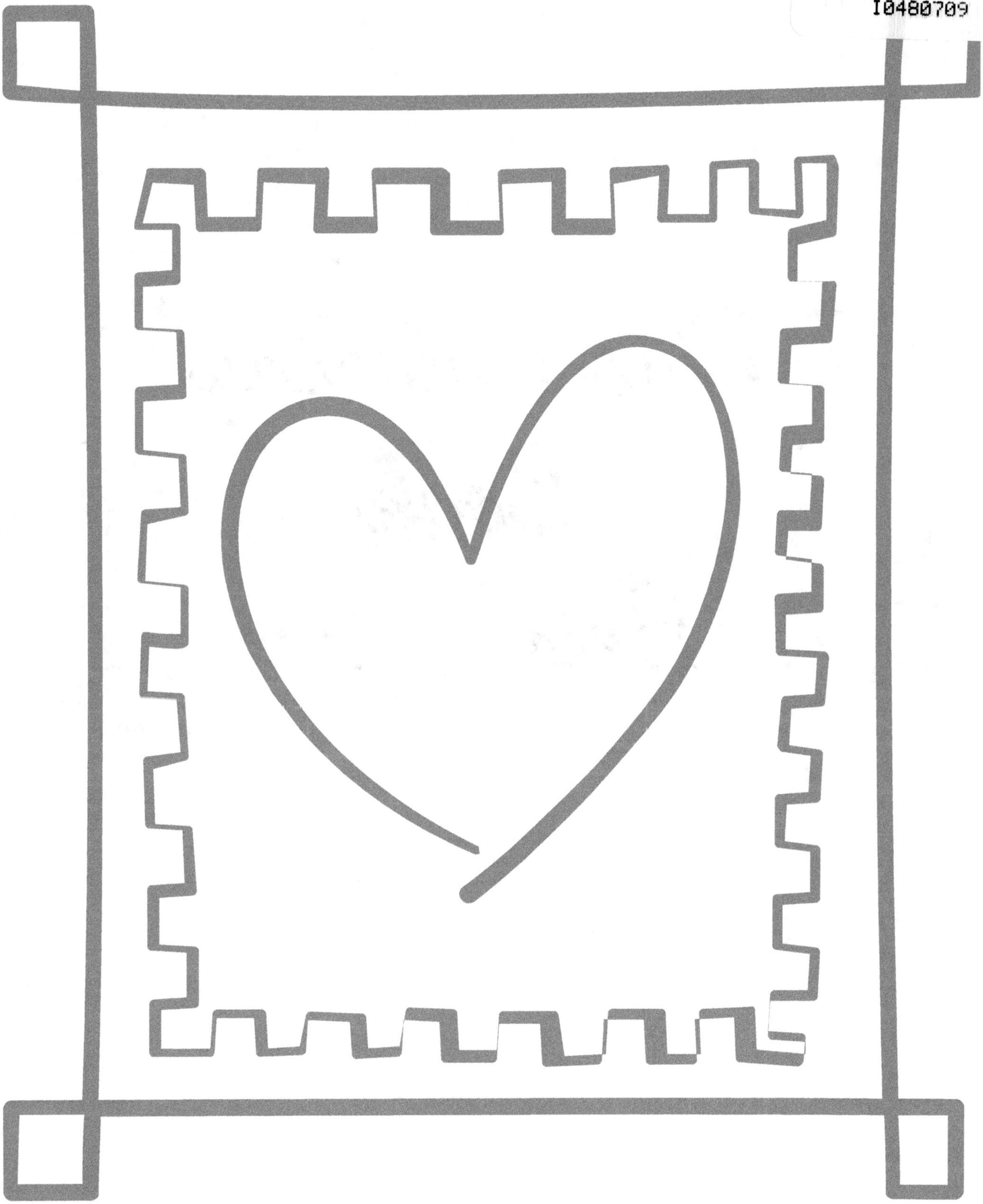

This Coloring Book Belong to:

_____

_____

_____

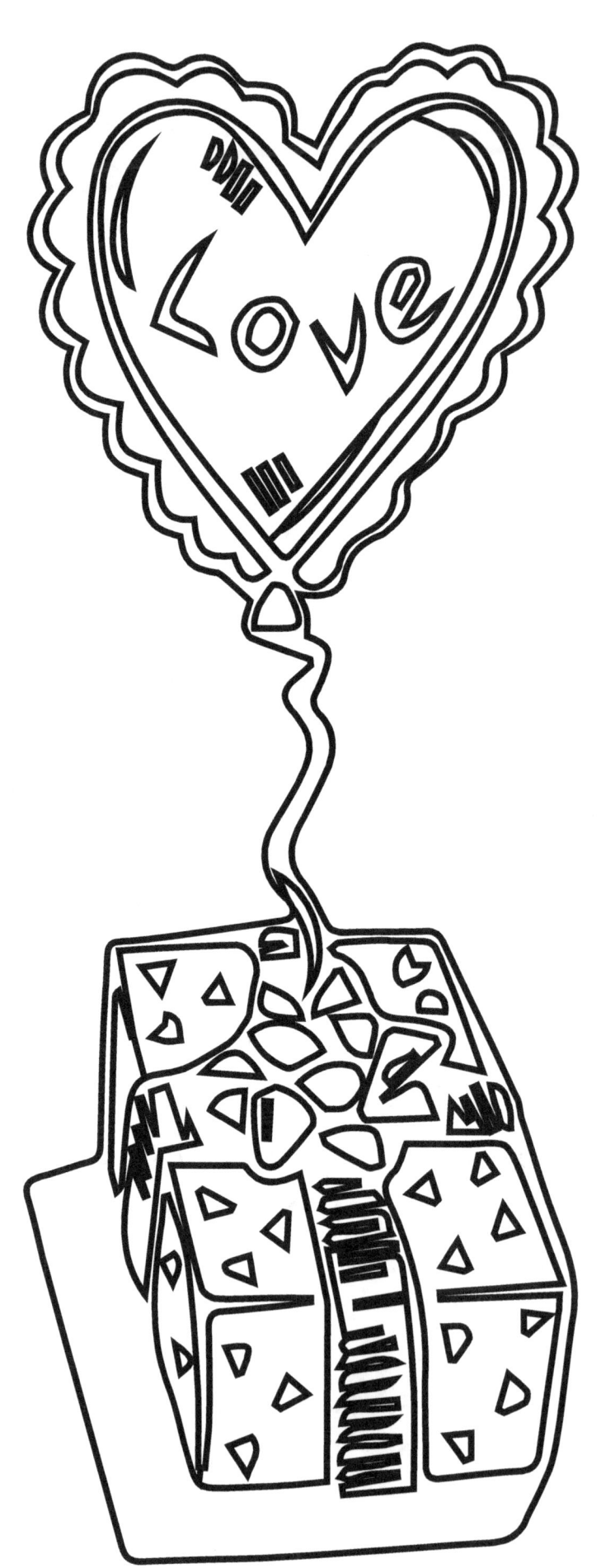

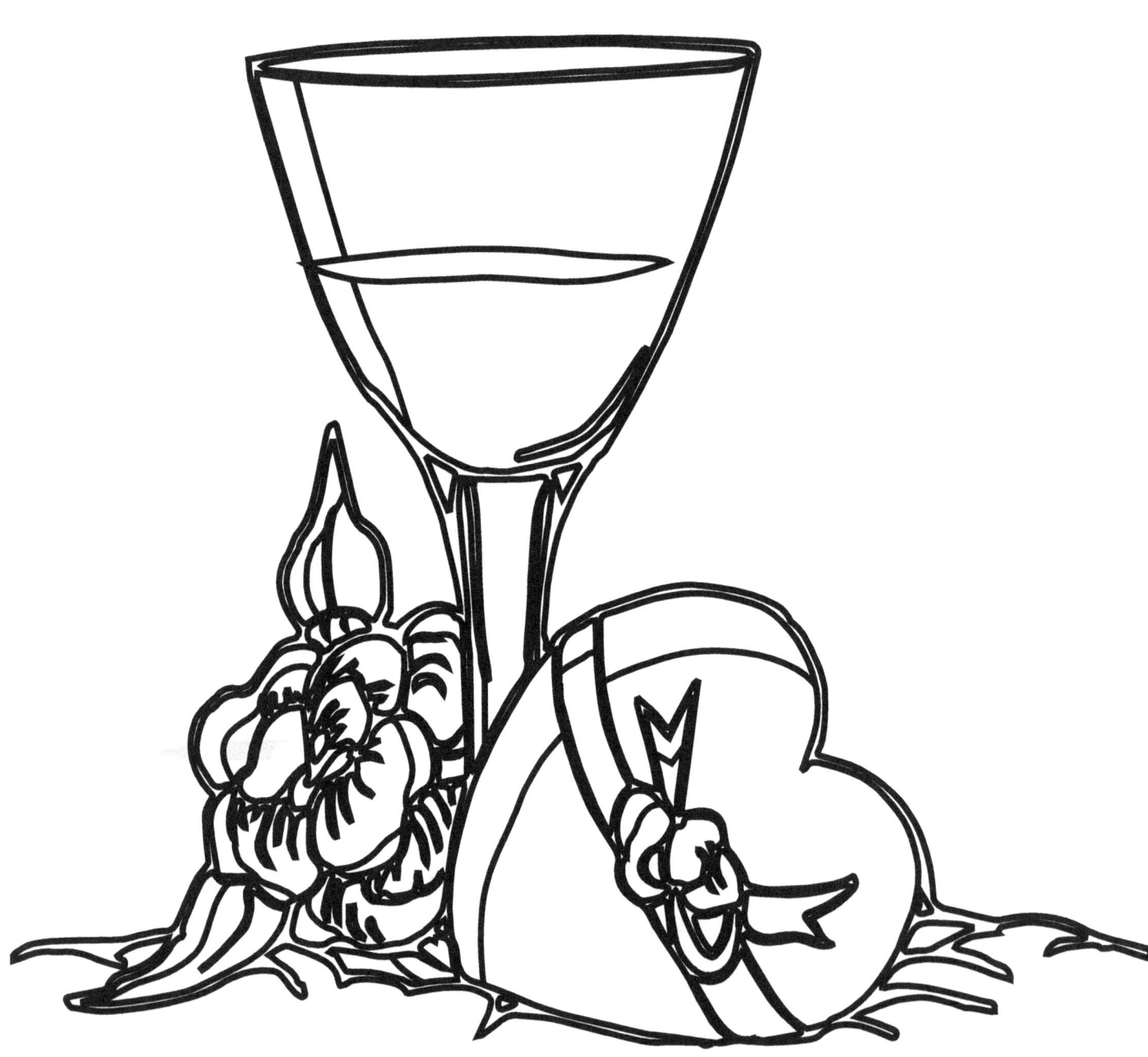

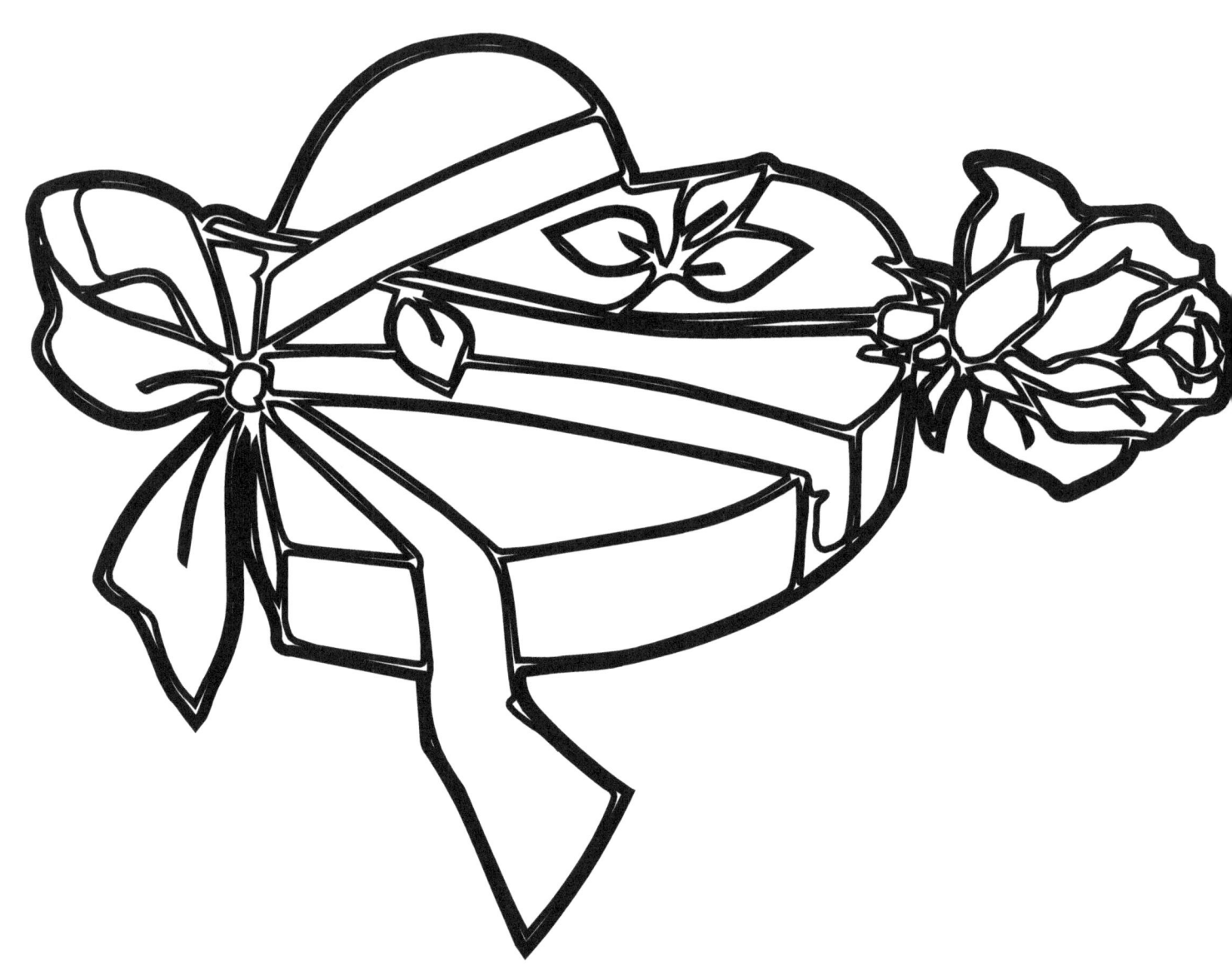

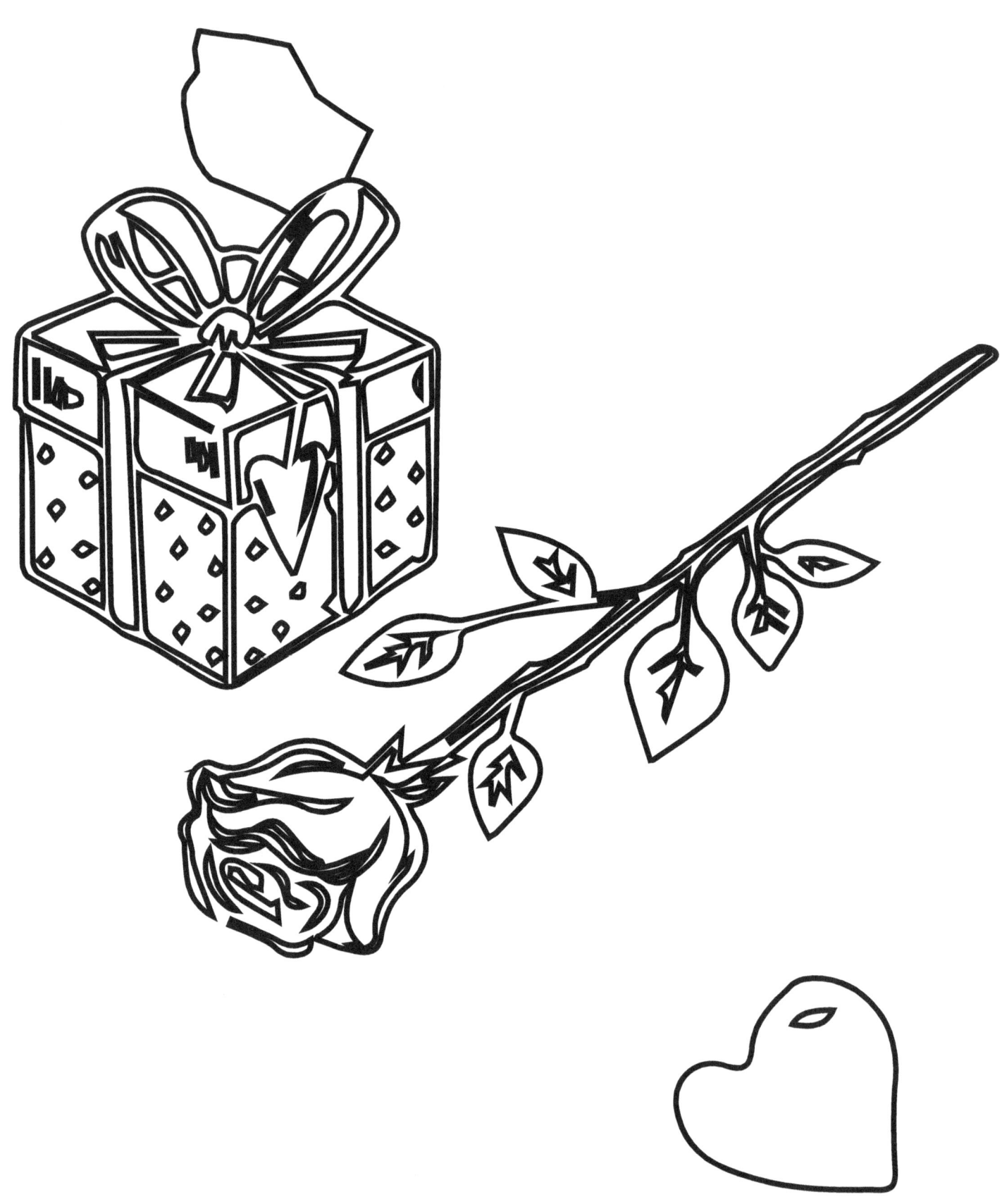

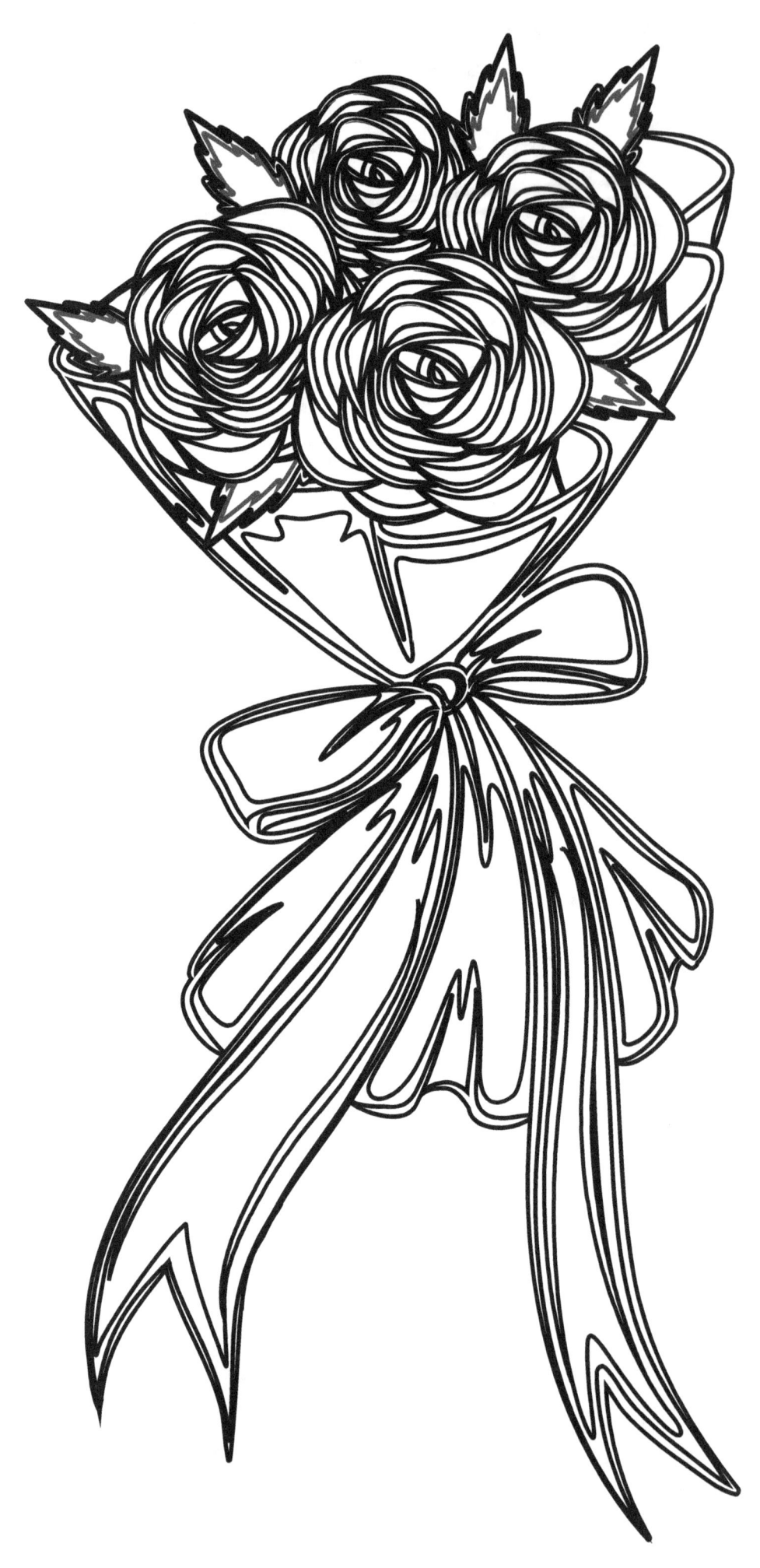

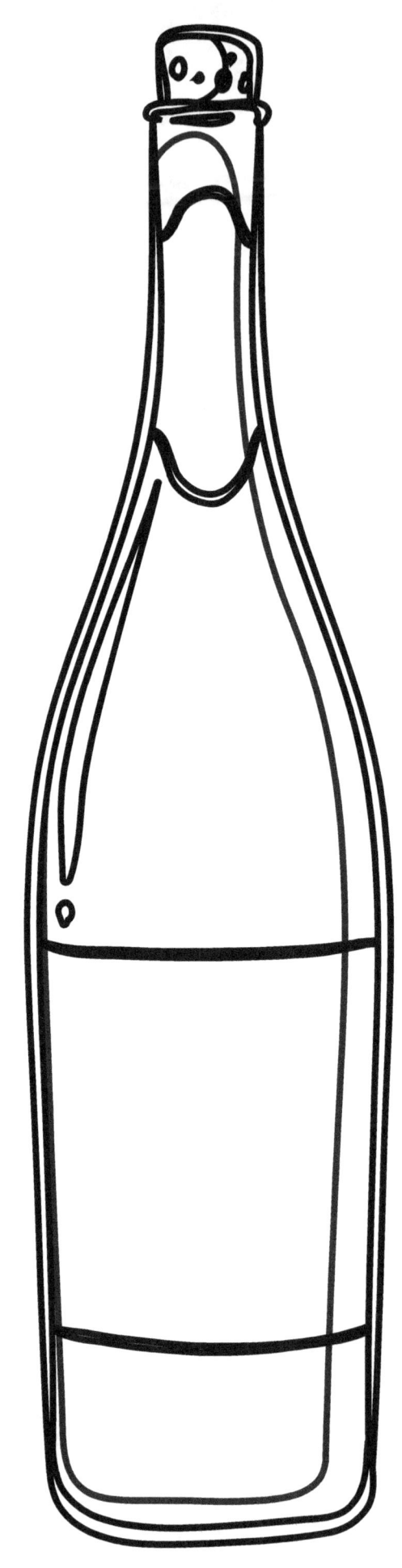

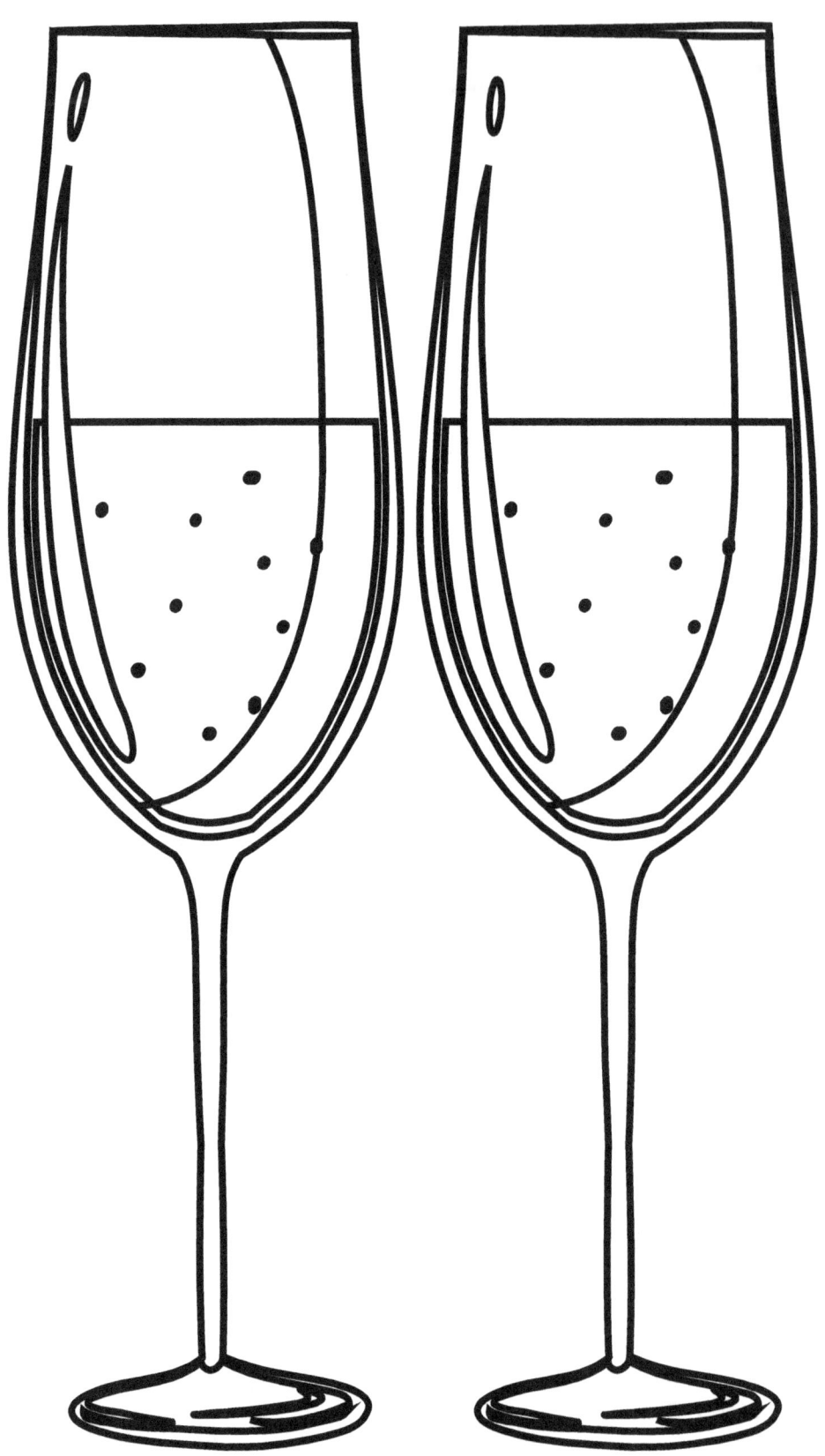

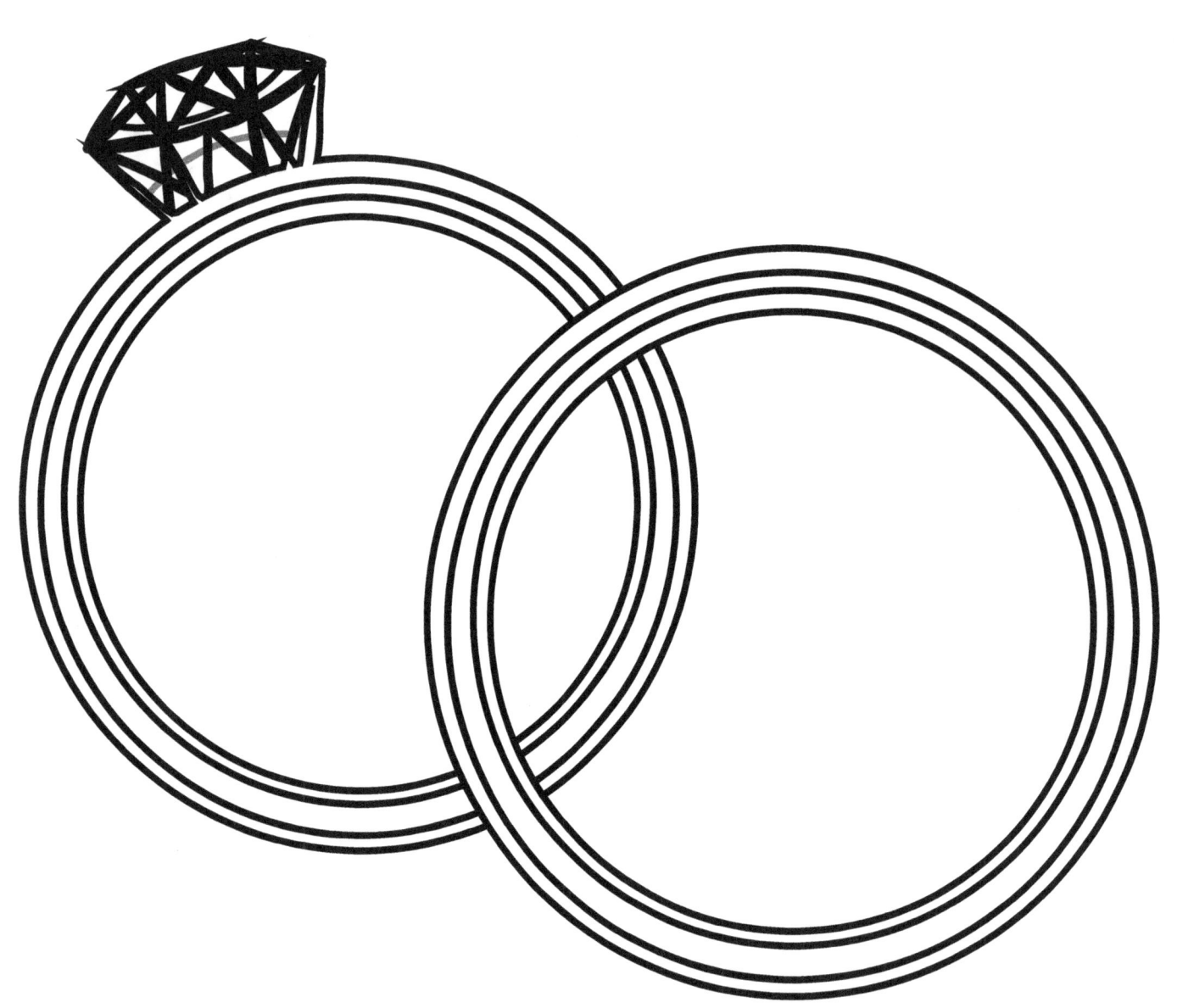

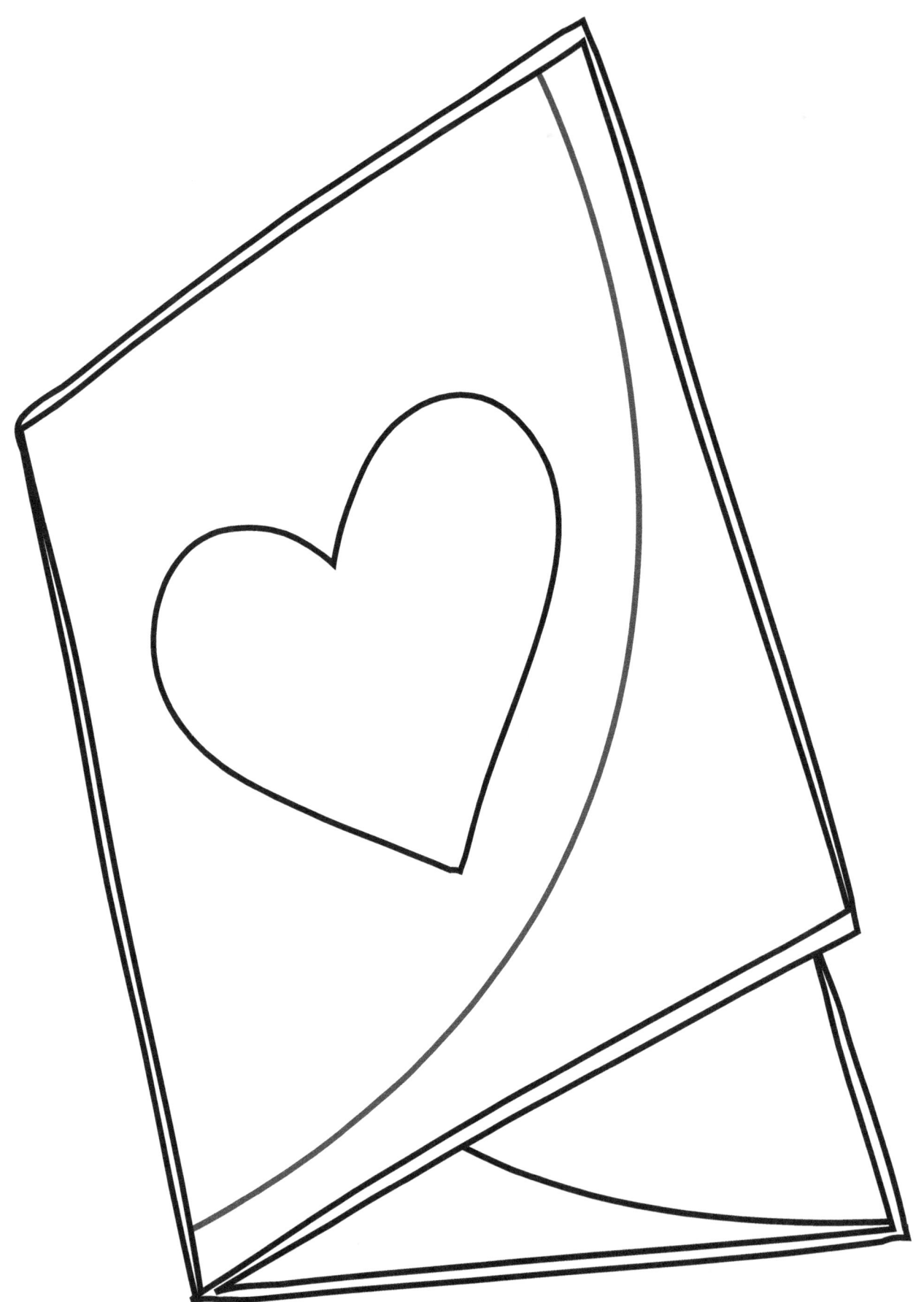

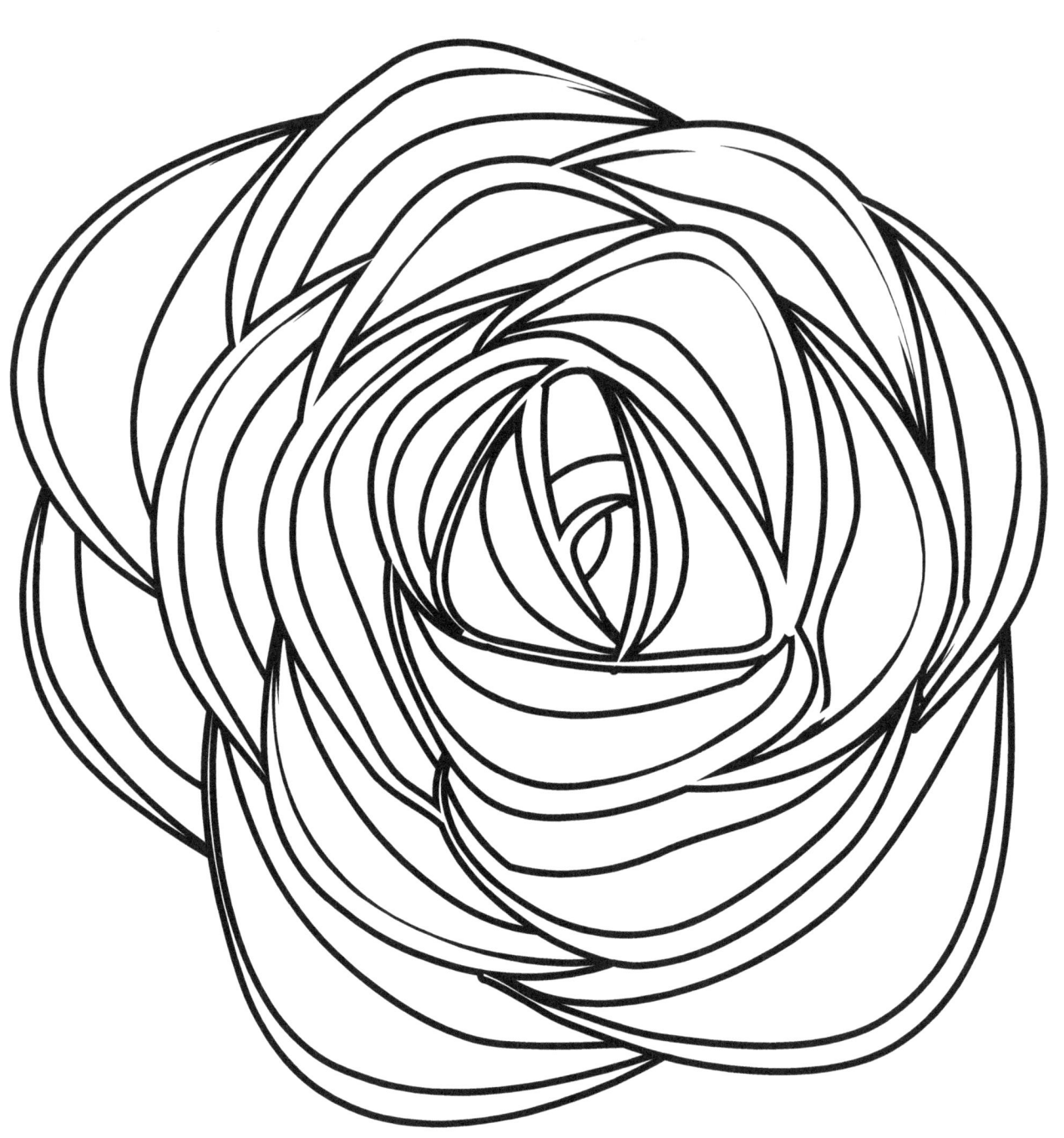

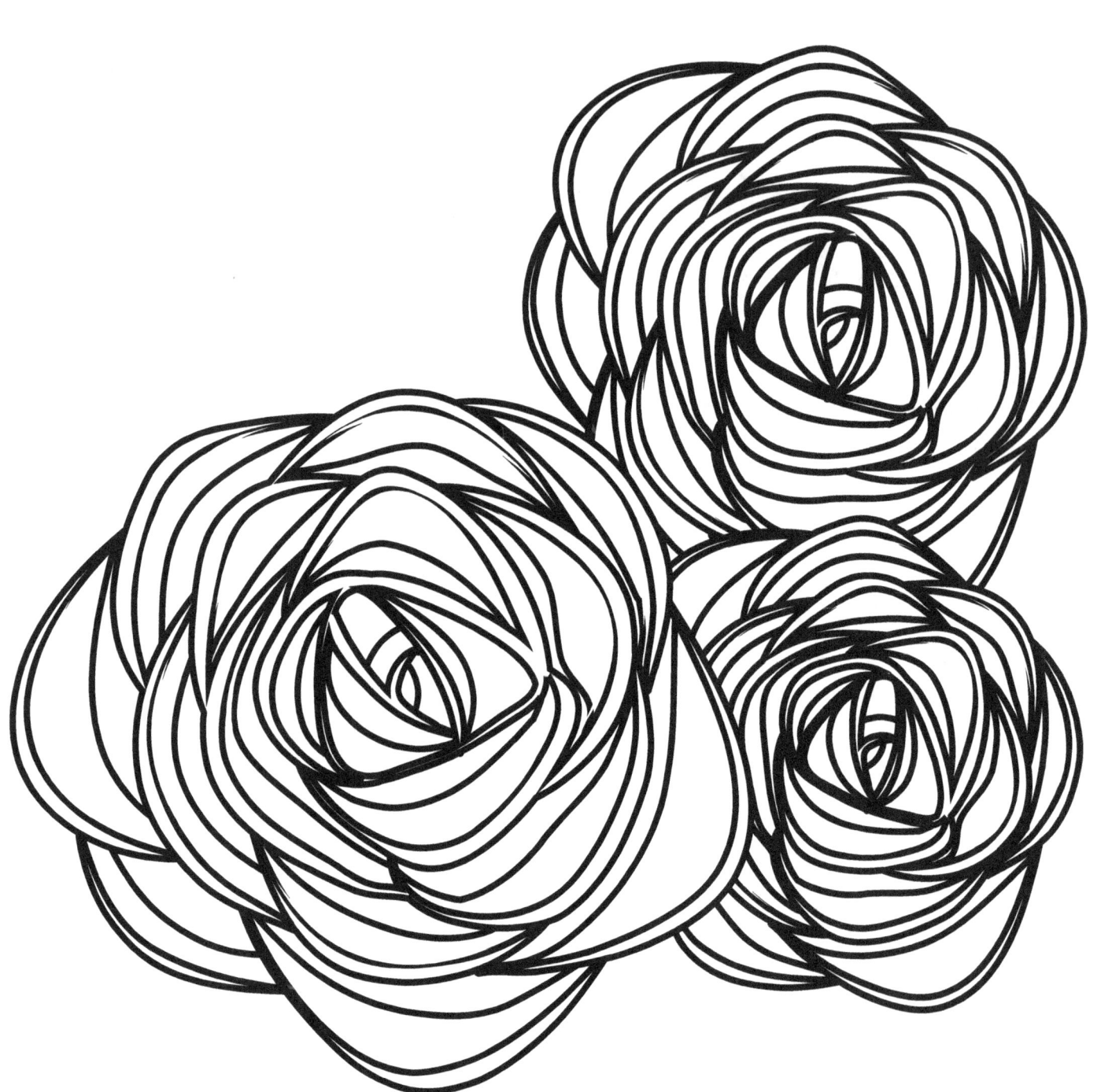

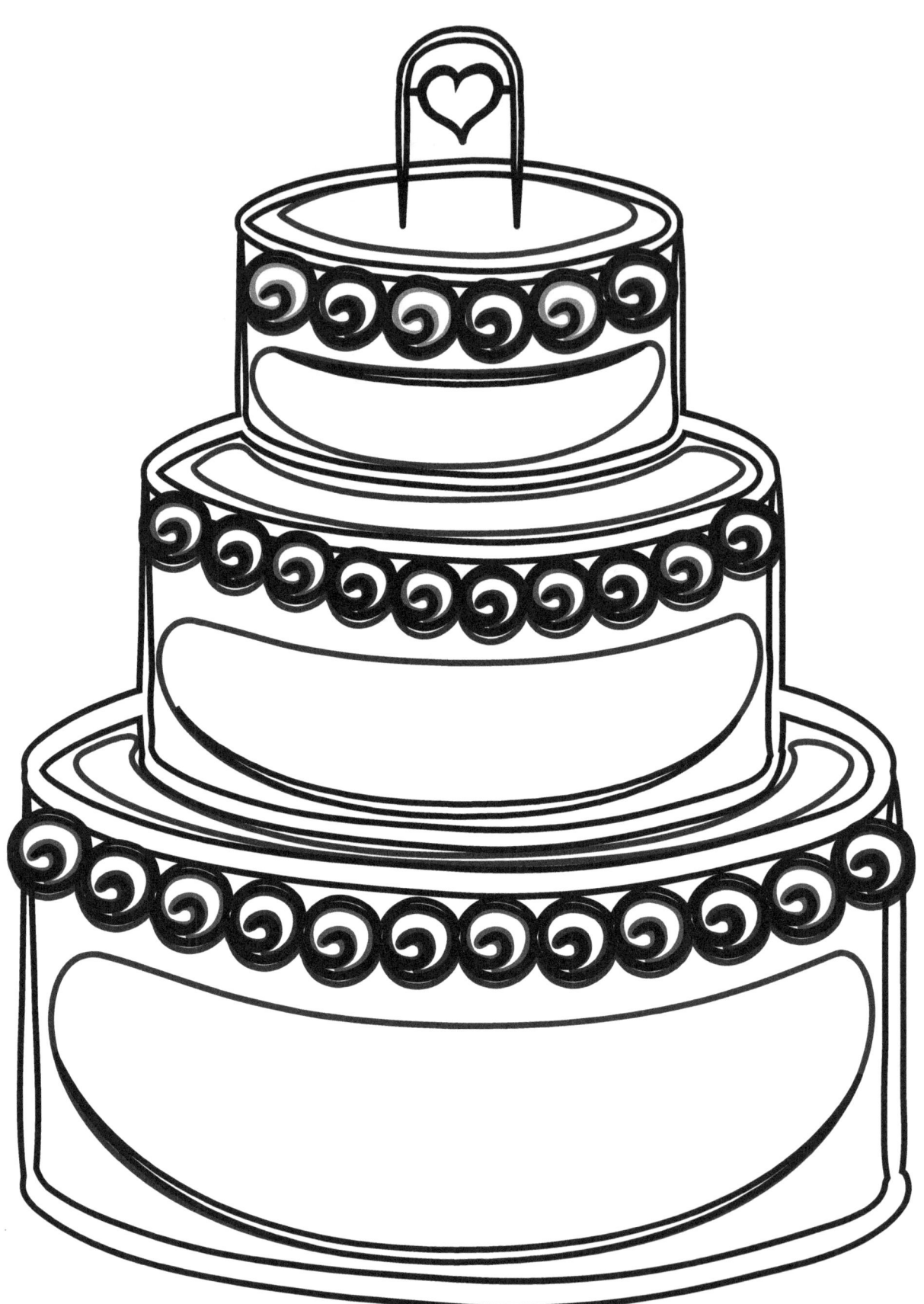

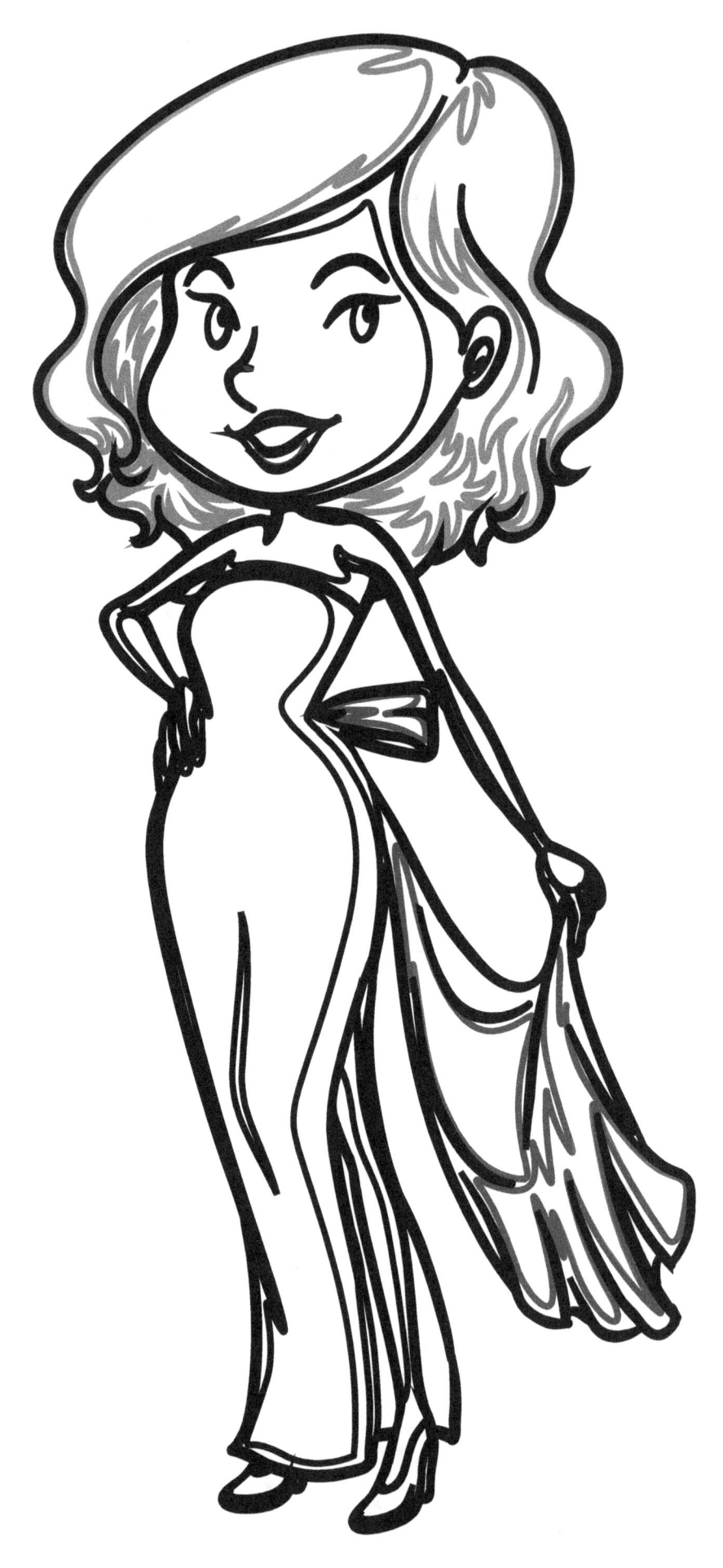

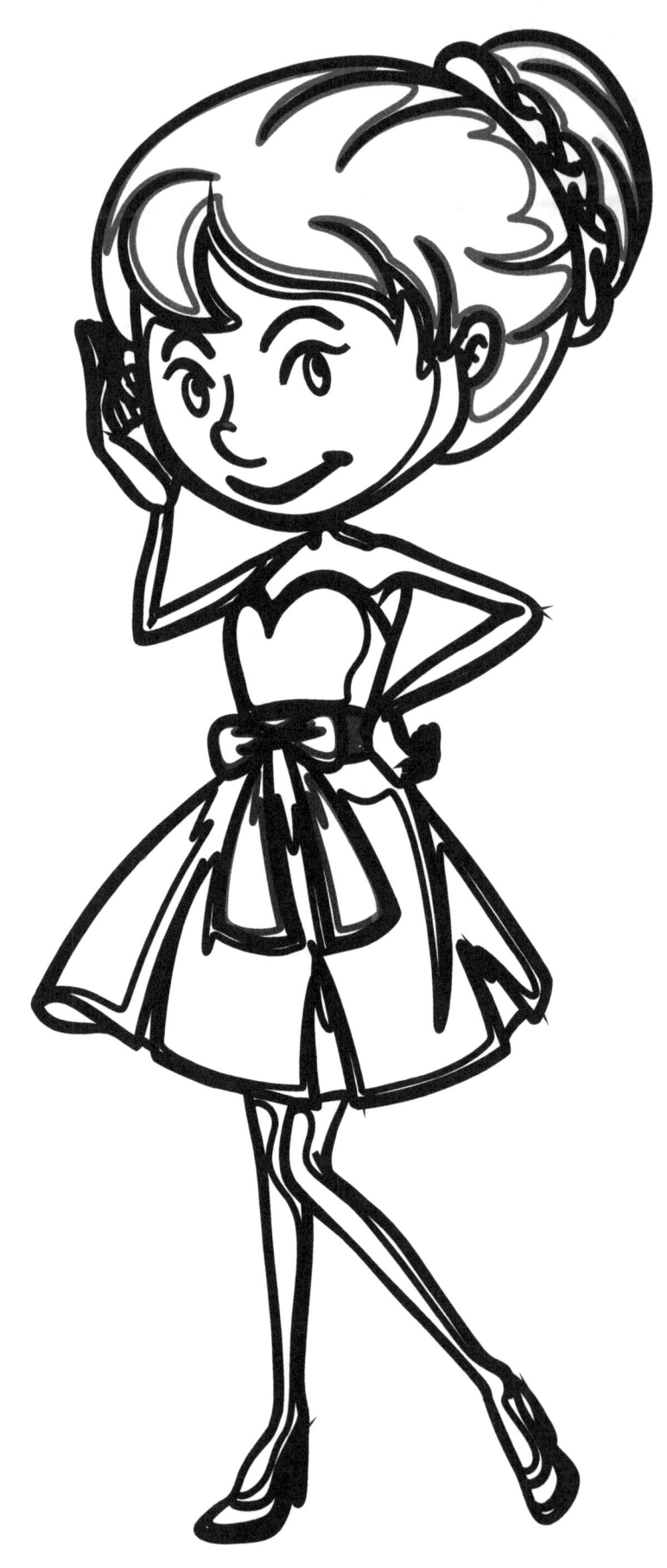

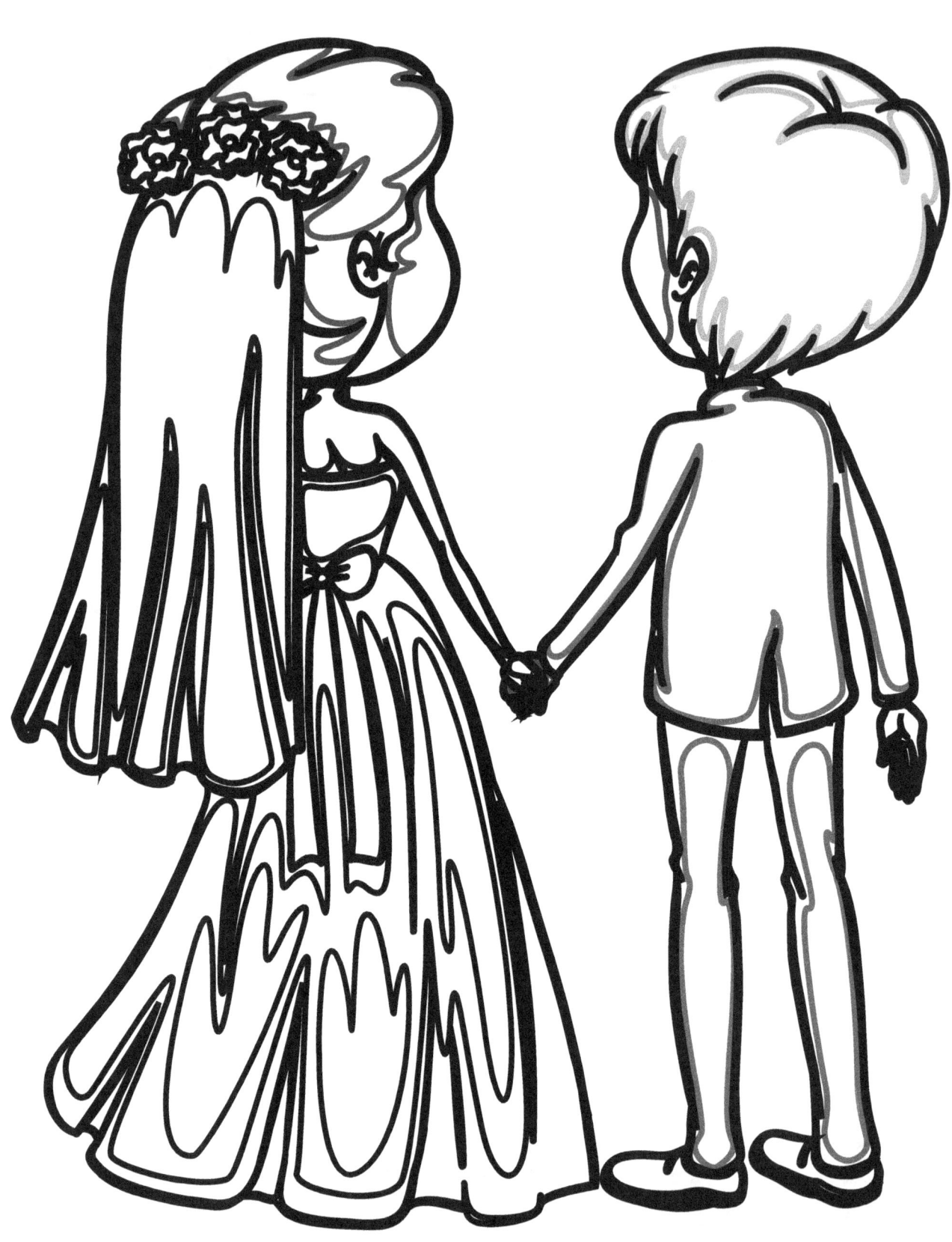

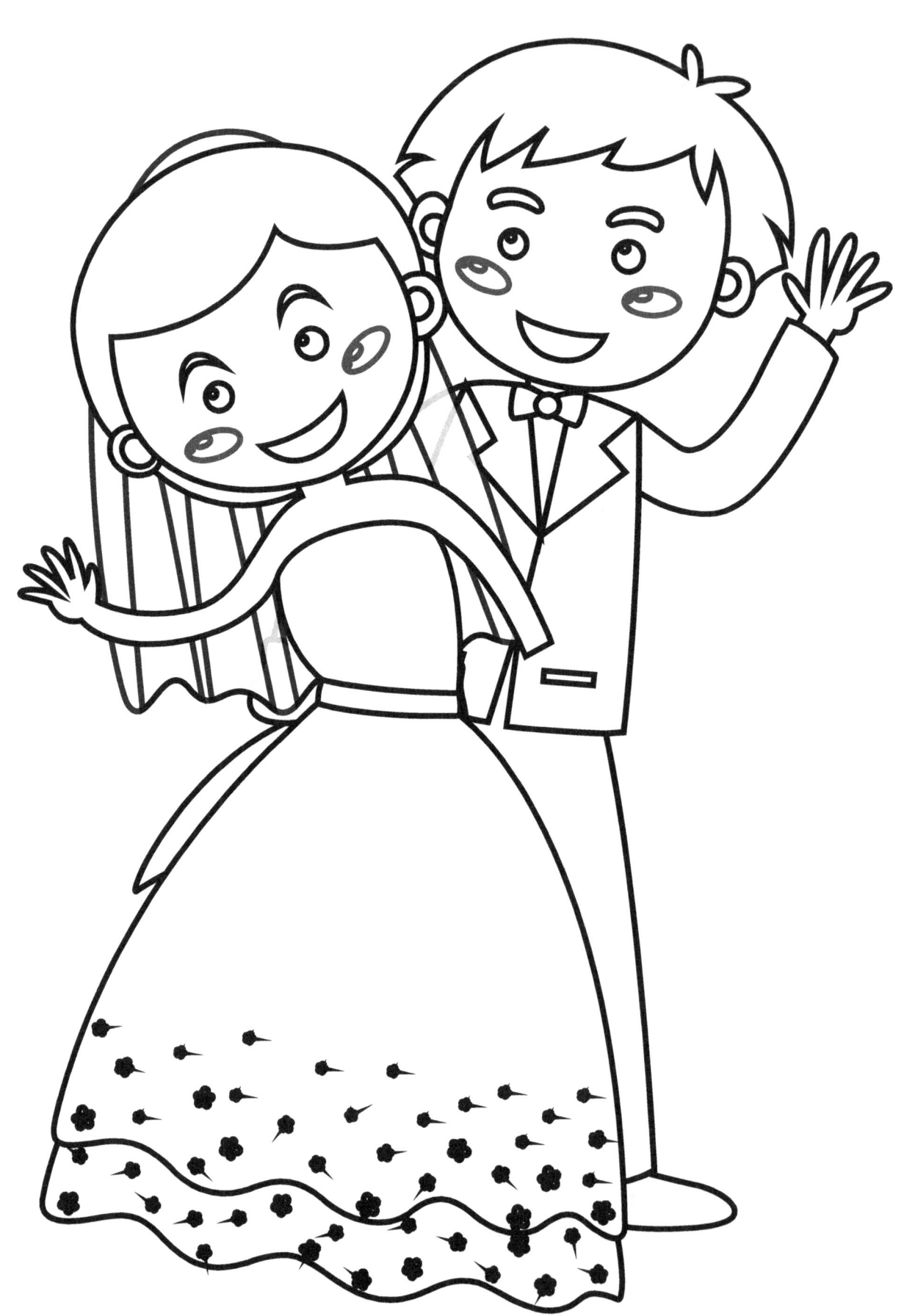

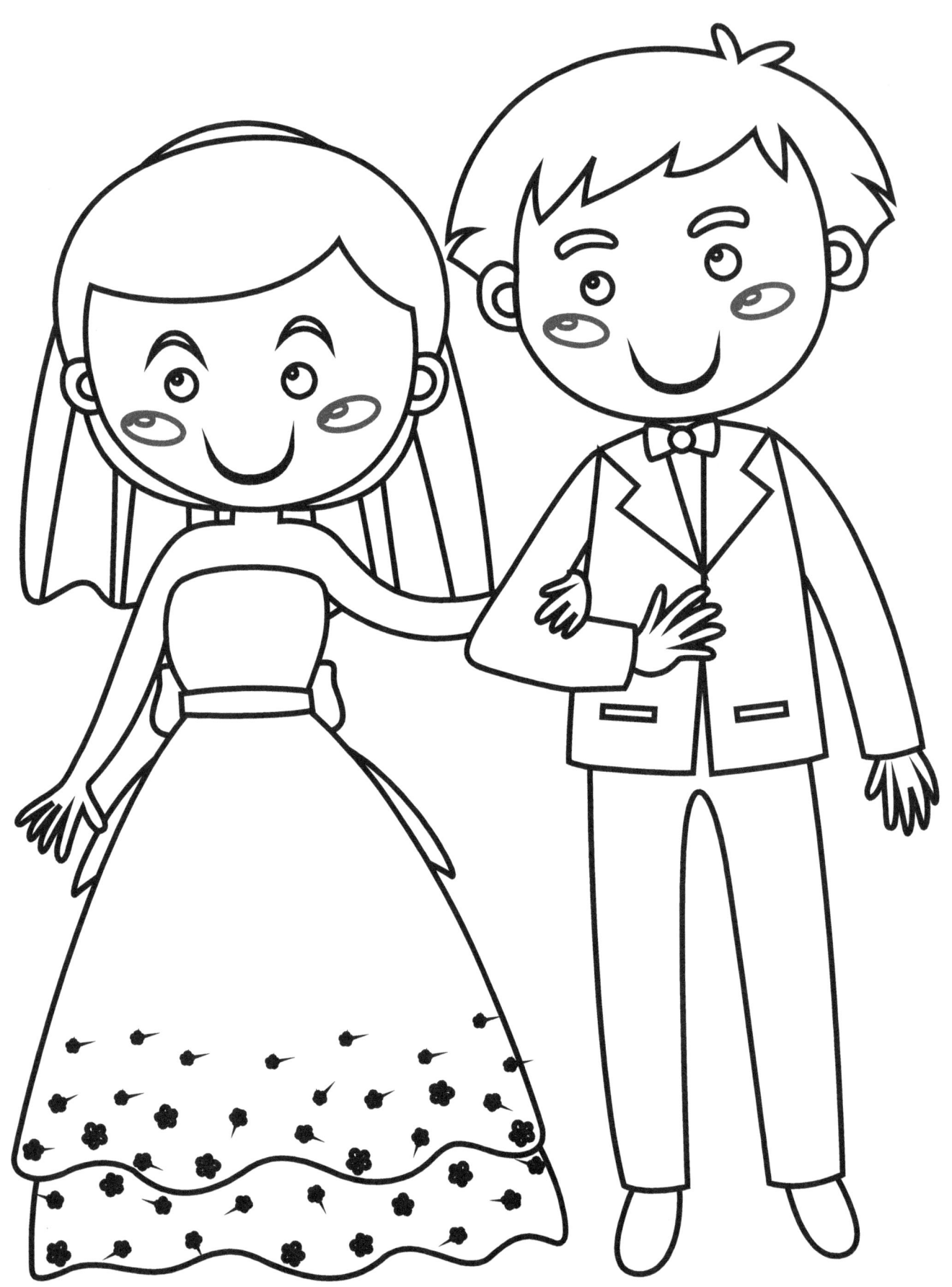

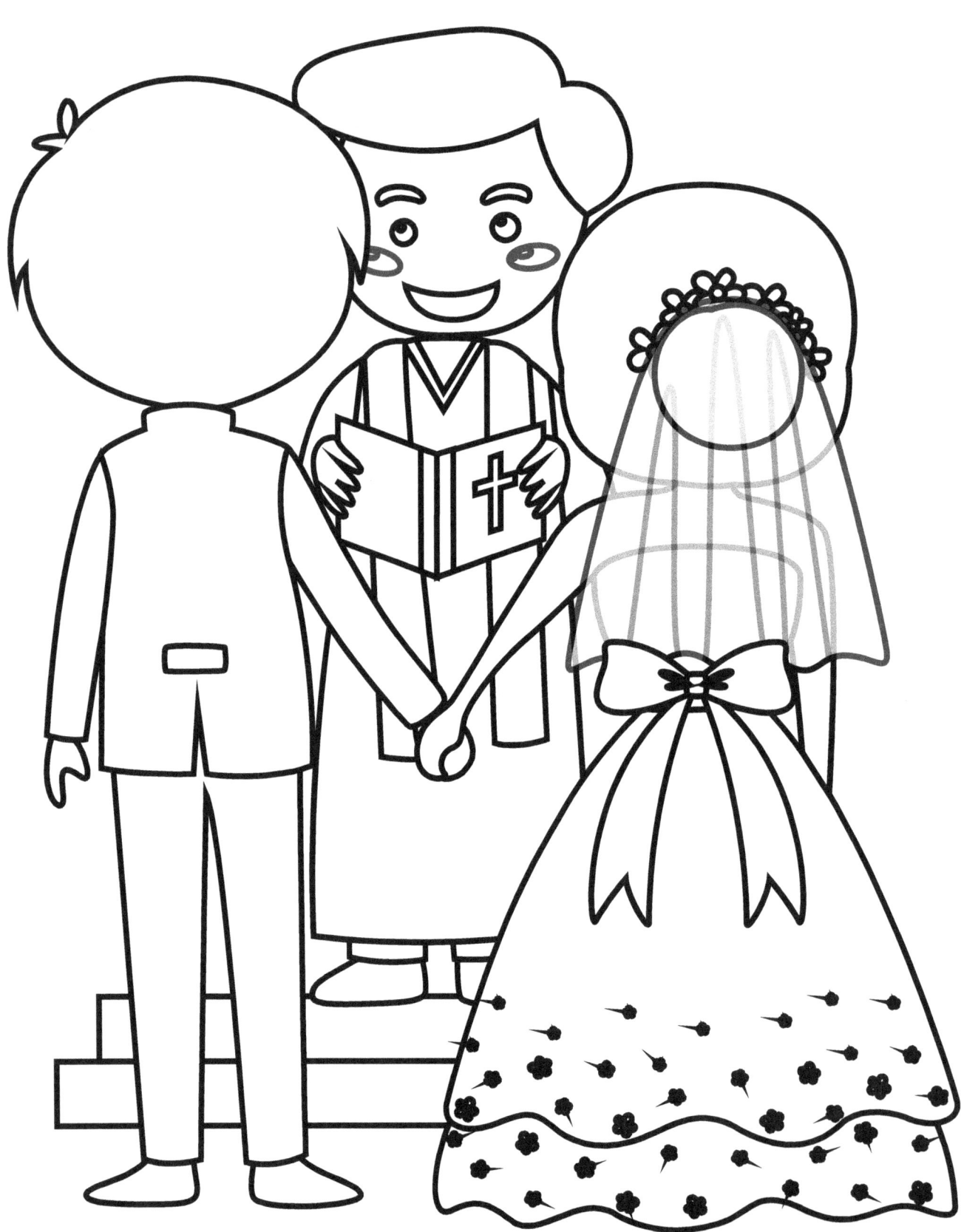

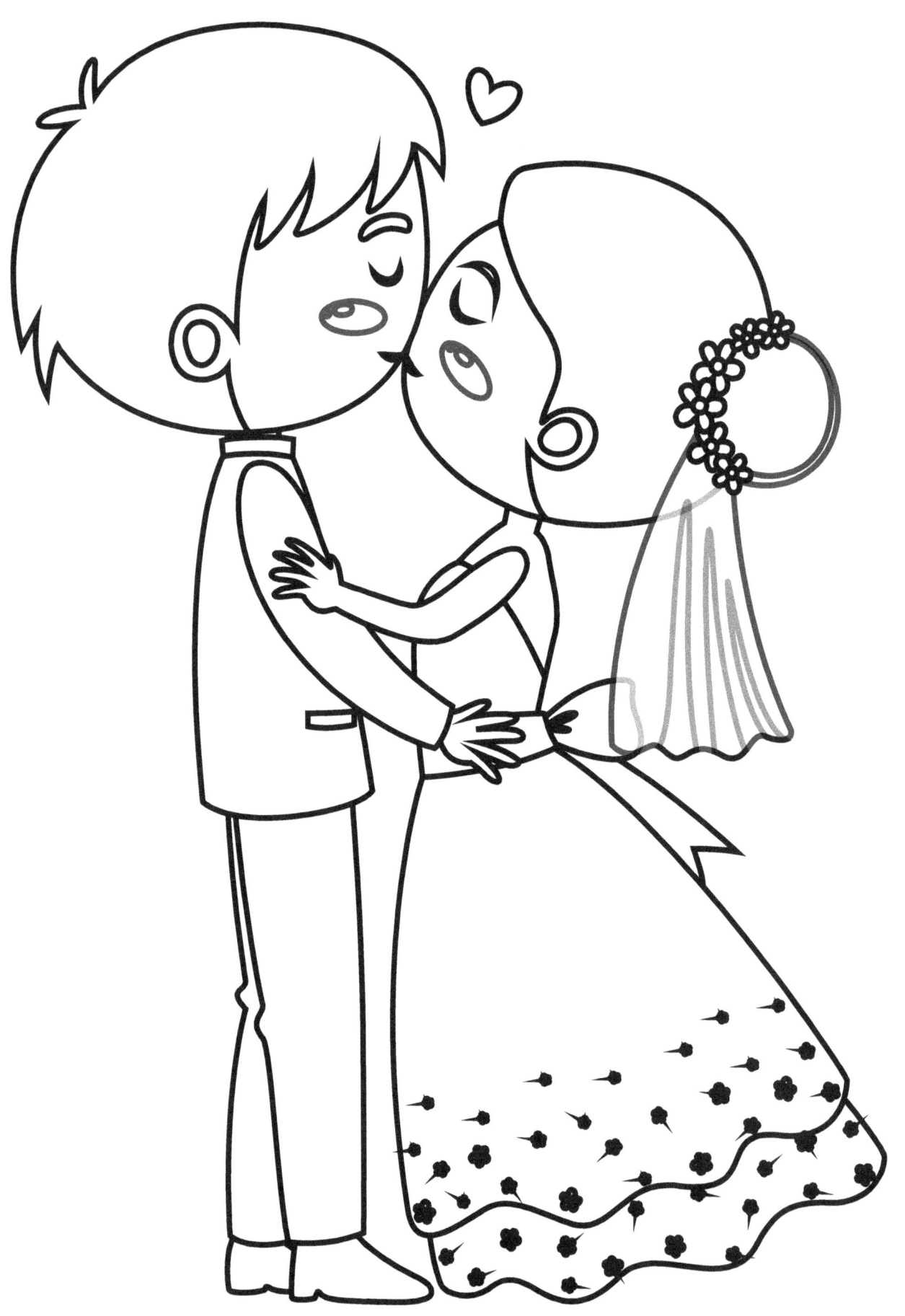

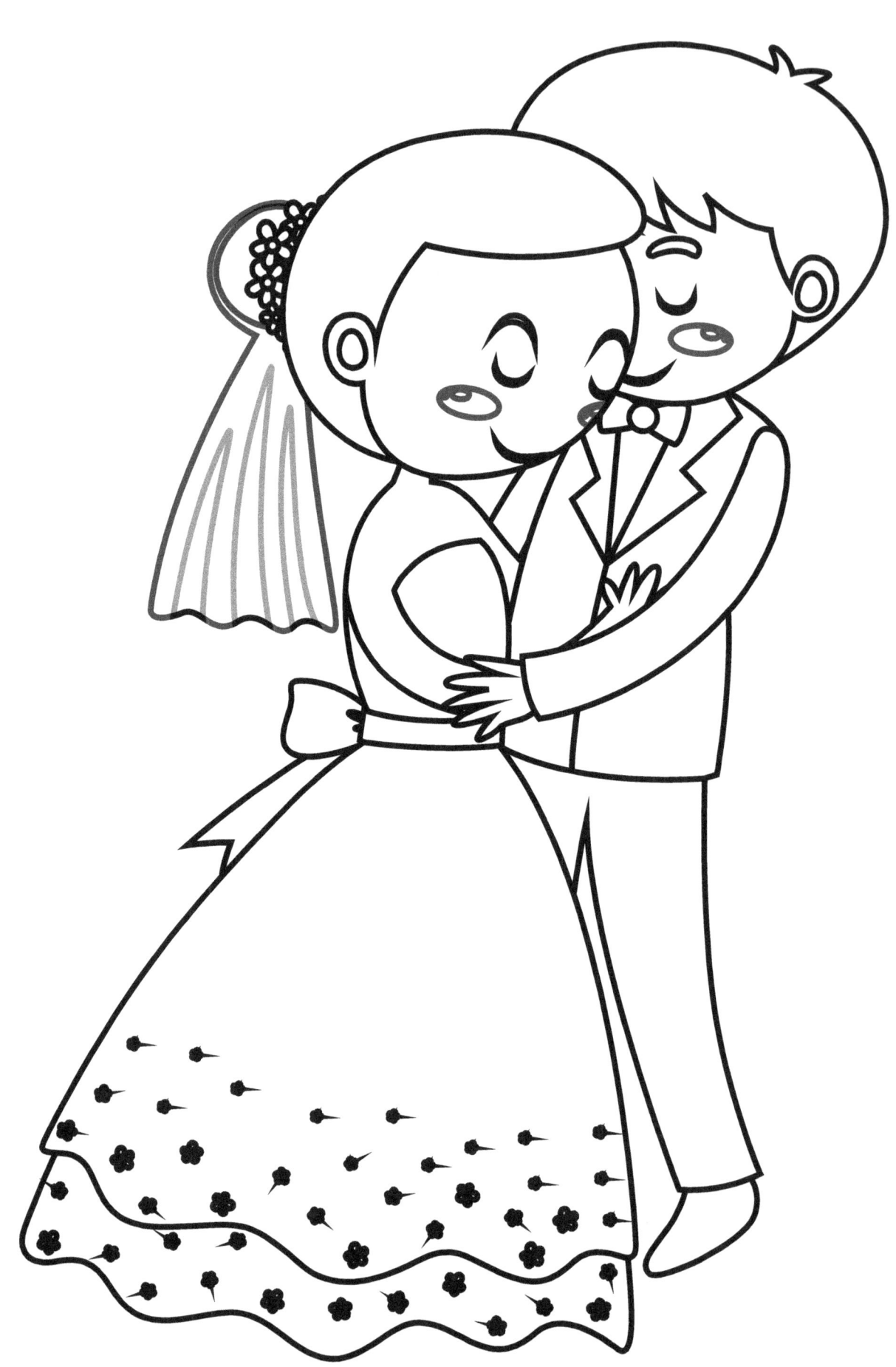

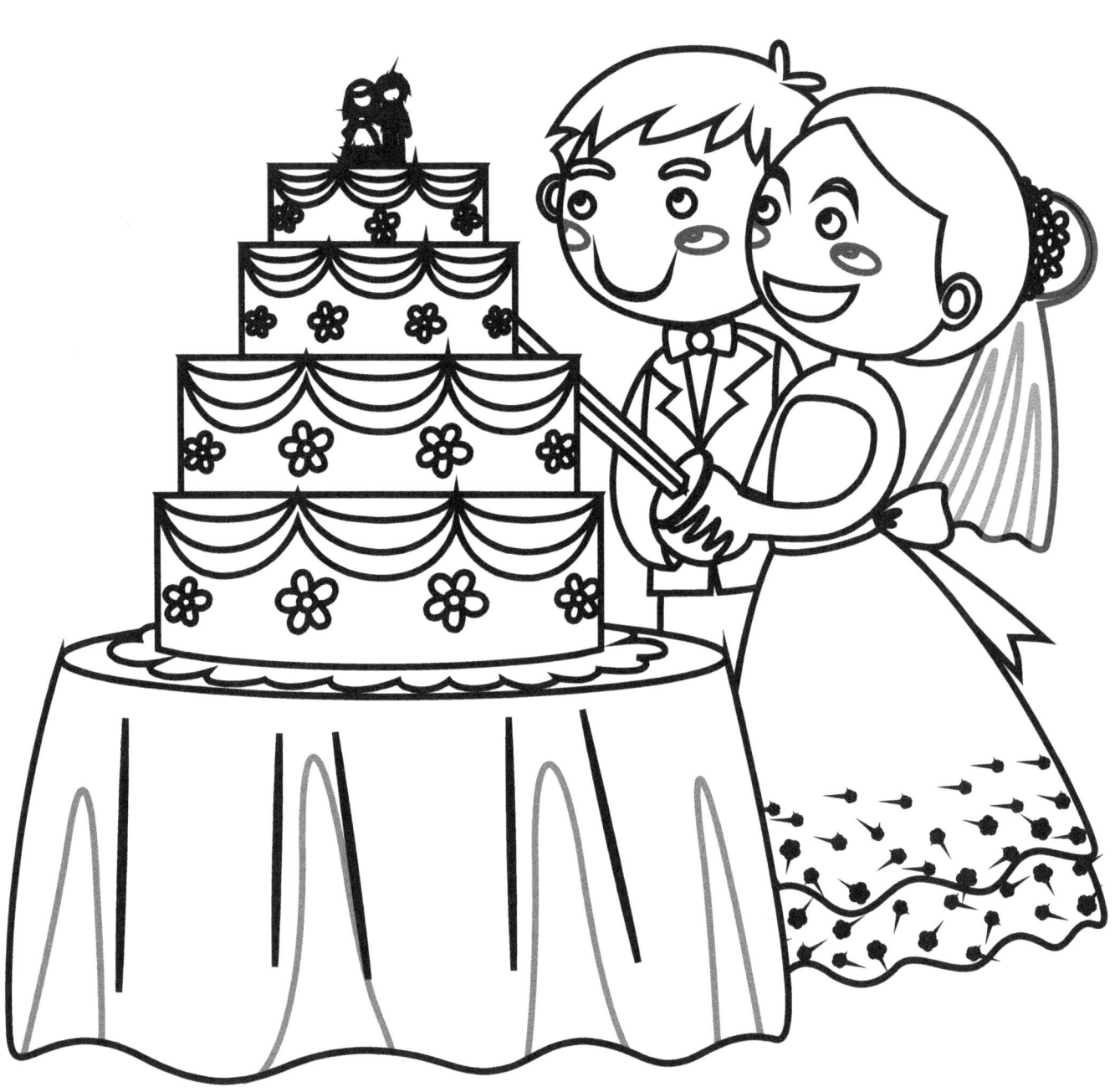

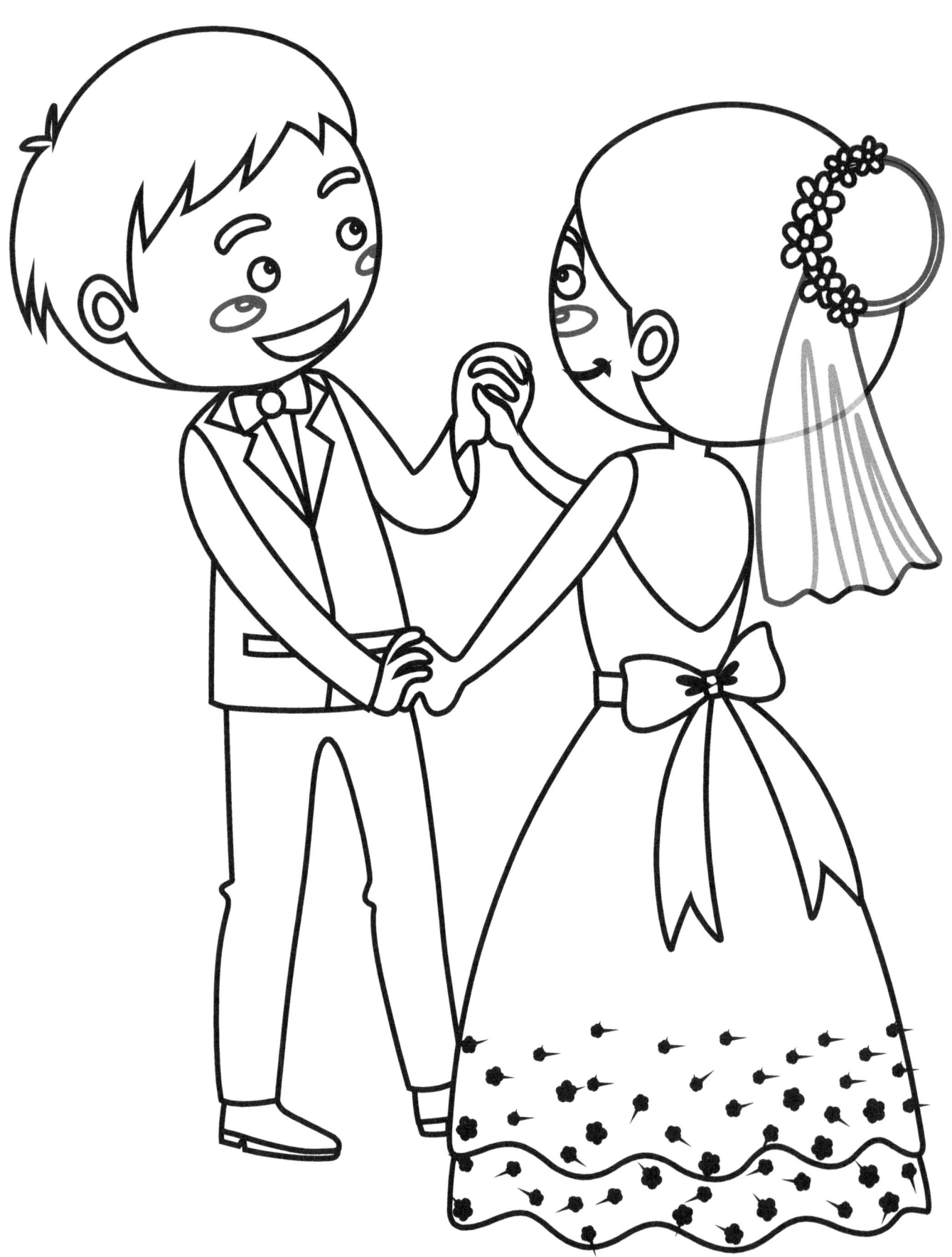

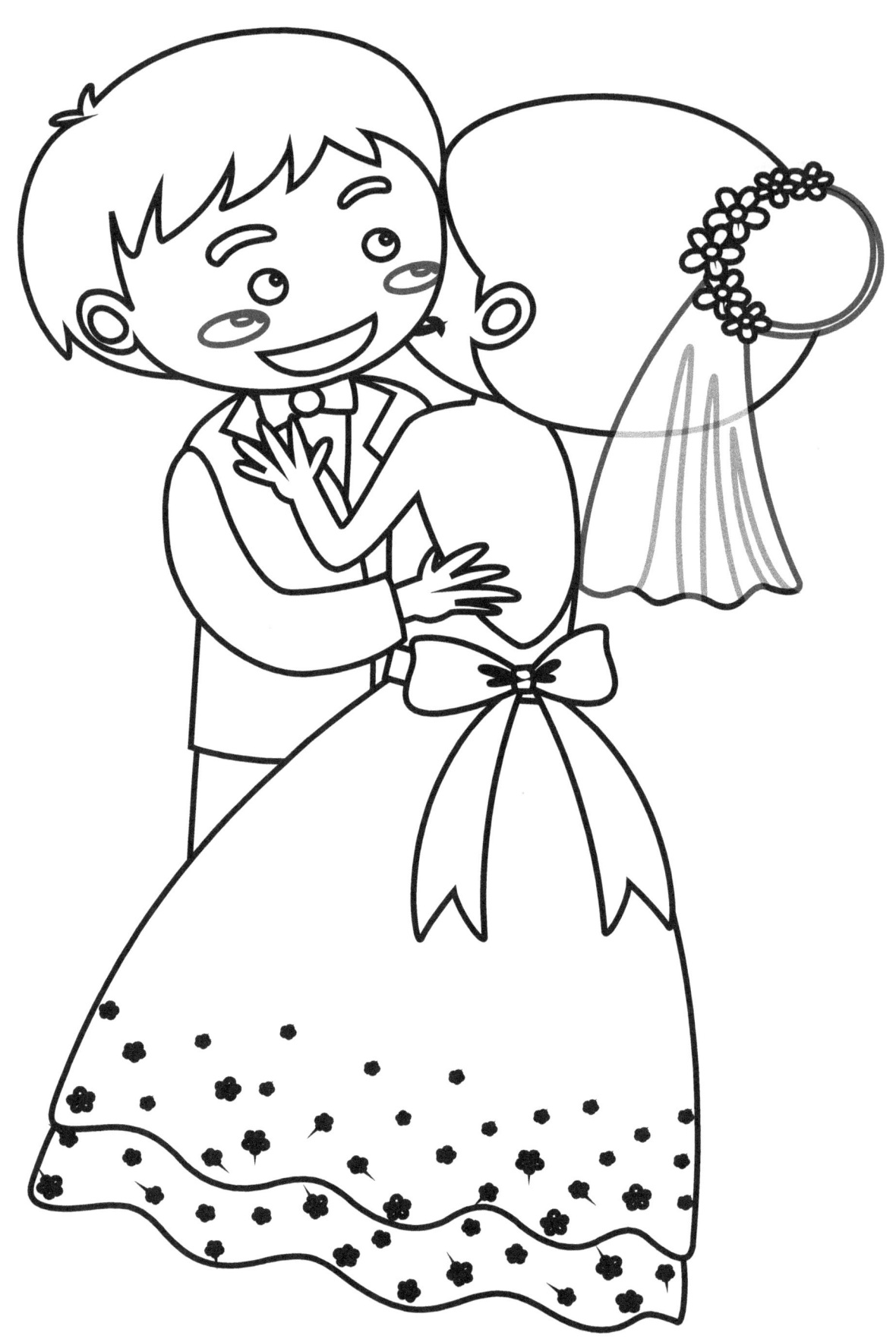

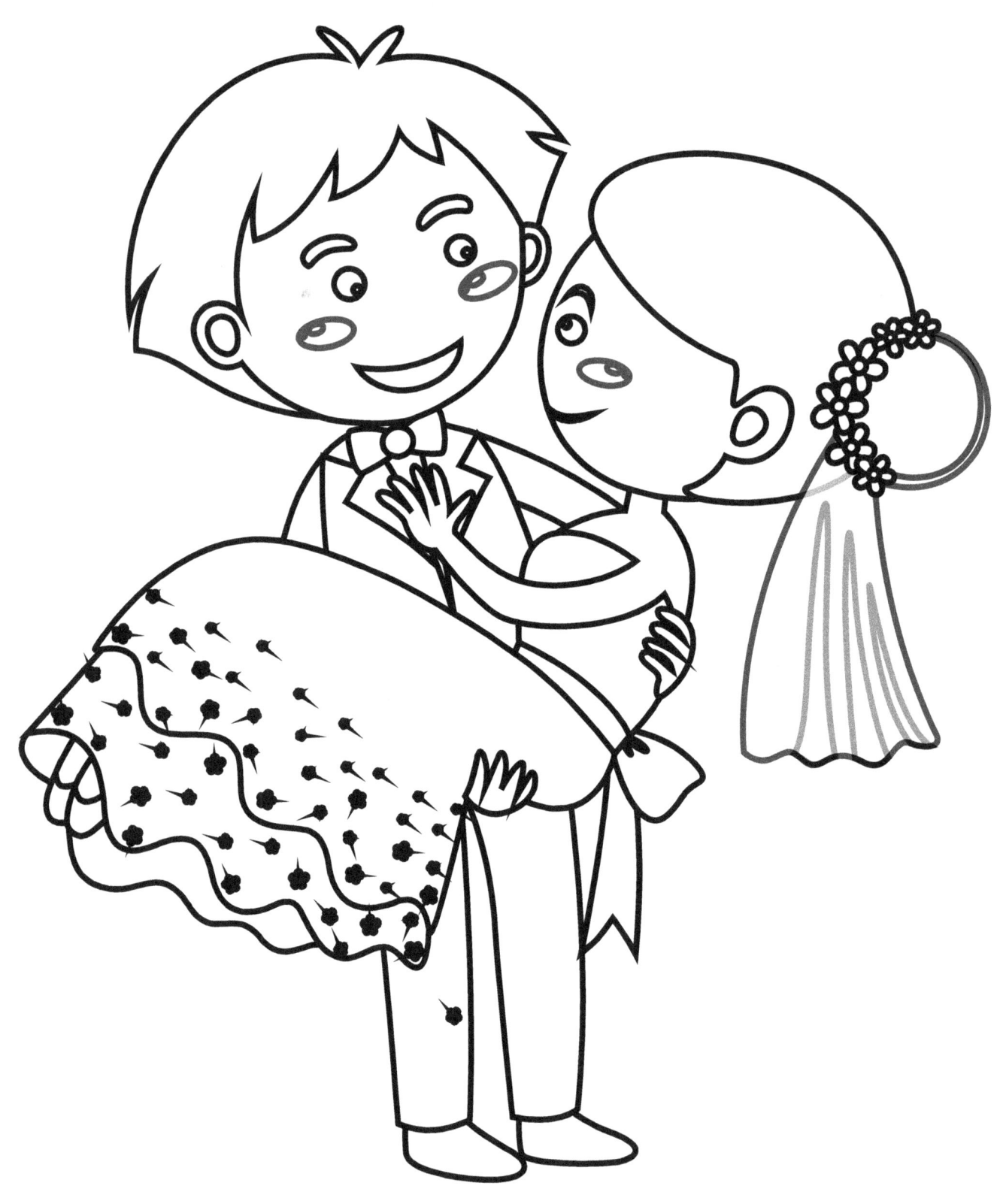

How to Color in a Coloring Book

Coloring books are fun for all ages. Although coloring is not generally considered to be very difficult, there are a number of methods and tips that you can use to help make your experience more enjoyable and successful.

Select your coloring utensils. Crayons and water-based markers are both great for kids. Gel pens are another fun option.

If you are using water-based markers that have become dried out, try reviving them by submerging the marker's tip in warm water for roughly five seconds

Find a surface to color on. If you are using a loose leaf coloring page you will need to find a hard surface to work on, while coloring books allow you more flexibility.

When using on loose sheets of paper, you may want to cover your work surface in newspaper depending on the coloring utensils you've chosen (markers may bleed through your paper and leave behind marks).

www.ingramcontent.com/pod-product-compliance
Lightning Source LLC
Chambersburg PA
CBHW081540220526
45467CB00010B/3273